from
Mary
Aug 1992

Traditional
Knitting

Traditional Knitting

Sheila McGregor

B. T. Batsford Ltd.

© Sheila McGregor 1983
First published 1983

ISBN 0 7134 4336 7

Typeset by Typewise Limited,
Wembley, Middlesex
and printed in Hong Kong
for the publishers
B. T. Batsford Ltd
4 Fitzhardinge Street
London W1H 0AH

Acknowledgement

I would like to extend my thanks to the Bergen
Museum; the Kelvingrove Museum, Glasgow; the
Burrell Collection, Glasgow; the National Museum
of Antiquities of Scotland, Edinburgh; the Scottish
Women's Rural Institutes, Edinburgh; Cecil and
Helen McGregor for generously allowing me to
photograph their collection; Dr Helen Bennett and
the Right Reverend the Bishop of Leicester for much
advice and information; John Lamotte for providing
invaluable illustrations; and all the others who have
helped in various ways.

SMcG
Edinburgh
September 1982

Contents

Introduction

Most of us today take knitting very much for granted, although we wear it from the cradle to the grave. And yet this simple skill, which can be taught to a four-year-old and which is so economical of resources that the poorest peasants have been able to exploit it, has stimulated royal envy, industrial espionage and Acts of Parliament, and has been the foundation of great trading empires. Today most of us wear knitting in one form or another most of the time as baby clothes, school jerseys, winter socks, underwear, Fair Isle and fisherknits, pullovers and polonecks. All of this derives, more closely than most people realise, from traditional knitting, the skill which queens shared with peasant girls when it first swept Europe only a few hundred years ago. Where did it come from? How did it spread and develop? Some of these questions are possible to answer; others we still have to guess at.

Today, although knitting is increasingly popular, it still suffers from a curious lack of respectability, though the last bastions are falling. Twinsets (with pearls) have been socially acceptable for all but the most formal functions for years but gentlemen wearing jerseys rather than a shirt and tie may still find themselves at an occasional disadvantage. How much things have changed since the days when Victorian sports enthusiasts first appeared in public wearing what their grandparents must have thought indecent striped underwear! Before then knitting was in much the same position as piano legs — necessary under-pinnings which were never mentioned in polite company and never allowed to show. Knitting has indeed gone through a revolution and come of age. Let us have a look at this youngest and simplest of the textile handcrafts.

The Origins of Knitting
Myth and Mystery

The history of knitting seems to have attracted more than its share of myths, unfairly it seems for such a humble, useful craft, as the true story is so much more interesting and informative. Some of these myths are pure invention; some contain the germ of a different mystery; some seem to be wishful thinking perpetuated in print, speculation drawn out far beyond the warranted conclusions. To mention a few of these knitting myths, in no particular order, it is said variously that Jesus wore a one-piece knitted garment, that the Spaniards from the Armada taught the Fair Isle crofters to knit (and even use the local dye plants), that the Aran patterns are thousands of years old and that the fishermen of Galilee two thousand years ago wore knitted caps. Many patterns are deduced to have religious significance. Some of these stories are charming, some curious; none are true. People interested in one-piece garments might investigate the world of primitive weaving, which contains many marvels.

The invention of knitting has been attributed to the Scots, the Turks, the Vikings, the Copts, the Arabs, the Irish monks, the Spanish and, by imputation, to the Indians. This, if nothing else, shows us what a popular invention it has been. It also probably reflects genuine folk memories of the way knitting expertise spread. If we restrict ourselves, however, to existing specimens of genuine knitting, a picture does emerge — not a complete one but true as far as it goes. Knitting is, of course, fragile stuff — little survives even one generation. The tools of the trade are simply thin sticks, formerly wood, bone or even quills, resharpened until they became too short to be useful and then thrown away. With no loom weights, no massive wooden beams, knitting has always been an evanescent technique.

Before we look at the little that has survived, we need to define what we are looking for — what is knitting? Today we understand this as a technique

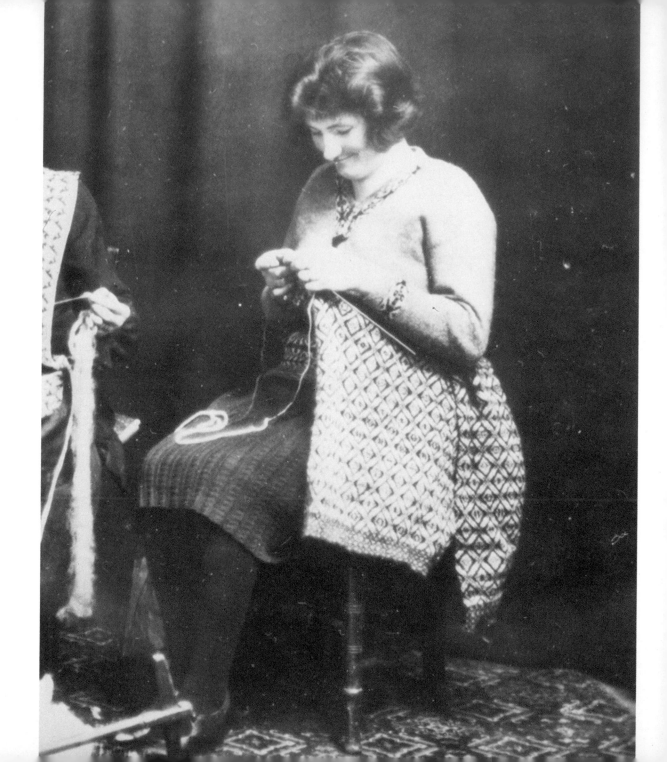

whereby we can construct flat or circular fabrics using needles or a series of hooks to hold a row of loops formed from a length of yarn which, for practical purposes, is endless (as the end of the yarn never needs to pass through the loop until the work is completely finished). Each of these loops normally is looped through the corresponding loop of the previous row and holds it; in turn it is held by the corresponding loop of the next row. In hand-knitting the right hand or the left may be used; both techniques produce exactly the same results and have been used simultaneously for hundreds of years in Europe. All of this has to be mentioned because there are quite a number of similar techniques which are not knitting and some not so similar which produce very similar results.

Crochet, for example, also uses an endless length of yarn and is indeed in many ways very like knitting. It uses only one hooked needle, however, and works one stitch at a time. Tunisian crochet uses one long hooked needle, to work along a row, picking up loops and then, without turning the work, to work back again. In consequence it unravels only along the row; knitting unravels up and down as well.

However, the earliest knit-look fabrics were darned or sewn, using a short length of wool which was pulled through each stitch. This technique has been recognised from the Stone Age in Switzerland and exists today in various degrees of sophistication from simple interlooping without even a needle to very complex interweavings still used by preference

Shetland knitter from 1930: a good advertisement for her own handiwork, she is knitting with two yarns, one in each hand. Knitting belt not visible. Her own jersey is much simpler than the one she is knitting which is probably for sale. (Photo from a postcard by J. Williamson, Scalloway, Shetland)

for working winter mittens in parts of Scandinavia. They call it *nålbindning*. The best yarn is said to contain very long fibres and to be barely spun. New lengths can then be wound in without an obvious join. *Nålbindning* is slow and complicated to work; on the other hand it is remarkably warm, comfortable and hard-wearing. That it was no cheap or primitive substitute for knitting is shown by the Finnish saying: 'He who wears knitted mittens has an unskilled wife'.

Most knitting today and, apparently, in earlier times seems to have used a plain stocking stitch. Mary Thomas in her classic *Knitting Book* describes a number of other stitches, crossed and uncrossed, which depend on hanging the stitches the 'wrong' way around on the left-hand needle, or knitting into the back of the loop instead of the front (which gives a twist), or both, when we get crossed eastern stocking stitch. Now it happens that a simple form of *nålbindning* gives a very similar result except that if the course of the yarn is traced very carefully it can be seen to pass through each loop before it is drawn tight. Hence much of the confusion over early 'knitting'. In fact any very old piece which is said to have been 'knitted' with a crossed stocking stitch was probably not and is certainly worth looking at again.

This is certainly true of the very nice little Coptic sandal-socks, worn in Egypt around AD 250, the precious maroon-and-gold fragment of 'stranded knitting' now in the Ikle Collection in Basle and many fine liturgical gloves of the Middle Ages in Europe. *Nålbindning* was very laborious and therefore very costly and, as Dorothy Burnham puts it so nicely in her *Textile History* article, 'would advertise the wealth of the wearer just as effectively, if rather more subtly, than rich jewellery'. It is ironic that some of the last examples of this ancient

technique are preserved alongside the earliest known European examples of the technique that replaced it: the knitted silk gloves of popes and bishops.

About AD 1100, perhaps earlier, a new fashion swept the Arab world. The dry air and warm sand of Egypt have preserved for us knitted socks with brilliant patterns that would not be out-of-place in High Street shops today. This seems to be the first true knitting known though this story is constantly

on the move! This break-through must have caused great excitement. We do not know if these patterned cotton socks were a local product or an import — some features suggest India as a possible origin, and Egypt certainly shows no direct antecedents — but we do know that they became

Shetland knitter from 1975: like the Shetland knitter from 1930, she is using 14 in. 'wires' or needles and knitting belt, a leather pouch filled with pony hair but has her two wools over the first finger of her right hand. The knitting belt leaves this hand free to move very rapidly while the left hand controls the stitches.

Below The style of these Afghan socks is at least 1000 years old and is still the only one known in a wide area of the Middle East, including Turkey and Afghanistan. In earlier days they were probably felted and worn as boot linings. In the absence of ribbing (a fairly recent development) the colours used are continued into a length of twisted cord which would be used to keep them up in place of a garter. They are first knitted from the toe to the top and then a length of wool is removed where the heel is to be fitted in.

lastingly popular in Egypt and were knitted and worn over the next several hundred years, through religious and political upheavals, as empires rose and fell. Local wool in bright colours — red, salmon pink, dark blue, light blue, green, yellow, fawn and turquoise — and white cotton have been found in patterned scraps.

Knowledge of this new technique seems to have spread very rapidly along North Africa and into Spain where the Moors were still established. In Burgos, the city of El Cid, a woollen cushion cover has been preserved, decorated with geometric patterns and stylised birds and flowers. The stranded technique used is the same as that used in Egypt and in Shetland today; even the patterns have much in common. Technicalities certainly have more to do with this than any historical or cultural

Striped and patterned socks enjoyed a deserved popularity in the Egypt of 1100 and 1200. The patterns are not quite as symmetrical as those knitted today in Shetland but show equal understanding of good pattern making. The geometric style, probably copied from a woven or embroidered original, has been adapted to avoid long toe-snagging loops on the inside. As in Shetland today, extra stitches have been added in one colour in the middle of long stretches of another to form part of the pattern, but at the same time keeping the longest stretch down to five stitches, about 1 cm (½ in.). The method used for the heel is still popular in the Middle East and can be seen in the Afghan socks (previous illustration). Although these patterns come from cotton stockings, similar patterns were also knitted locally. Are these a cheap import from India, as the cotton yarn would suggest? Or were they a new fashion? We may never know.

connections; a good pattern in AD 1100 is still a good pattern today, as any Fair Isle knitter will confirm. Indeed from the technical point of view the Egyptian patterns are more sophisticated than the Spanish.

These early knitters may possibly have used hooked knitting needles. Mary Thomas reports the finding of such needles in a twelfth century Turkish tomb and their use in the twentieth century by the shepherds of Les Landes, salt marshes in southern France (also noted for wearing sheepskins, but no socks, and walking around on stilts to see further over the flat pastures). Early needles are sometimes shown as being sharp at one end and quite blunt at the other. If anyone wonders how on earth people knitted with hooked needles, one should take a couple of crochet hooks and try a small sample! Provided the hook is in the right hand and the blunt end in the left, it is perfectly easy. If the Continental method (with the yarn controlled by the left hand and hooked through the stitches by the tip of the right needle) is used, a hooked needle is a positive advantage. In fact, if the Tunisian crochet which we mentioned above is an older technique than knitting, which seems very likely, one can imagine someone trying to produce circular work with a number of long hooked needles and suddenly discovering that they were knitting. How much quicker to go around and around! And how much more elastic and adaptable the result! None of these

Natural wools. Top row from left: *Welsh Black Mountain; five natural Shetland and Gotland yarns (Antartex).* Centre: *fleece from Herdwick in four shades — dark brown, red-brown, grey and white.* Bottom row from left: *Shetland; fancy Jacob; blended Jacob; Herdwick; Swaledale; Black Hebridean.*

Herdwick

A hill and mountain breed found mainly on the Cumbrian fells. This sheep produces a fleece from light grey to almost black, according to its age.

R. W. PERRI...
BRITISH WO...
NORWOOD C...
HALIFA...

Pure Swaledale

This sheep is to be found in the Dales and Fells of Yorkshire and in Cumbria. The fleece is a light brown shade, hardwearing and retains a great deal of its natural oil.

R. W. PERRI...
BRITISH WO...
NORWOOD C...
HALIFA...

experiments with hooked needles, incidentally, produce a crossed stocking stitch.

From Spain, knowledge of knitting probably diffused through the Church. Spain was not only the cradle of knitting in Europe; silk culture was another of the many benefits brought to Europe by the Moors (in addition to such disciplines as mathematics, chemistry and philosophy). Silk, with its fine, long fibre, and knitting have always been natural partners. One of the earliest applications of silk knitting was in liturgical gloves, and prominent and powerful people lusted after Spanish silk gloves in a most un-Christian way. One must bear in mind that *nålbindning* was still in use and possibly even more desirable during the period of overlap. However, knitting was known in Italy by the thirteenth or fourteenth century, in England by the fifteenth and in Scotland slightly later, as far as we

know. It is said to have reached Iceland (probably from the Netherlands) in 1560 and Scandinavia later still.

This very fine and prestigious silk knitting remained a greatly prized luxury for some considerable time; indeed, it would still be a luxury today. Although Edward IV had knitted garments listed in his wardrobe, the splendid and powerful Henry VIII appears to have found it difficult to get hold of silk stockings unless, as the chronicler Stow puts it, a pair came by great chance out of Spain. As the woollen stockings available to him were probably coarse and drab, he usually wore the traditional cloth hose, bias-cut from fine material, and seamed at the back. The seams in stockings today still imitate this feature. By the time his daughter Elizabeth reigned, the finest hand-knitting could be done for her by the ladies of her court. This break-through, which made her both fashionable and independent of Spain, may have had something to do with an early industrial spy, an English apprentice called William Riley. A contemporary writer relates that this young man saw a pair of worsted hose in the house of an Italian merchant in London, borrowed them and succeeded in copying them. Felkin in his history of *Machine–Wrought Hosiery* comments that worsted (which was finely spun wool) must have been known long before; these must have been silk hose. I rather believe that their value lay in the technique, not the type of yarn - earlier hose may have lacked proper heels or some other refinement. Whatever happened was obviously of great importance and from then on England did not need to rely on imports of this very fine knitting.

Silk was rare and valuable throughout the sixteenth and seventeenth centuries and most knitting was done then, as now, in wool. This had developed so widely during the fifteenth century that by 1488 the hand-knitting lobby had enough political clout to get a very favourable Act passed which controlled the relative prices of felt hats and knitted caps. Even more partisan was the Cappers' Act of 1571 which imposed the wearing of knitted caps on all Tudor gentlemen below a certain rank, on pain of a substantial fine. These fulled and shaped caps can be seen in many a Tudor portrait, including those of the king himself. An Act of 1552 mentions knitted gloves, sleeves and petticoats as well as hose. This substantial commercial workforce enjoyed the protection of Queen Elizabeth and were so powerful that the earliest knitting-frame, invented by William Lee in 1589, was banned in this country and first exploited abroad, not the last British invention to suffer that fate.

At the top end of the market we now find professional guilds of knitters. They were more active on the Continent than in Britain where commercial hand-knitting always seems to have been a large-scale cottage industry. Their 'masterpieces' were patterned woollen carpets, about two metres or six feet square, the traditional bed-rug size and probably intended for that use rather than the none-too-clean floors of the time. Apprentices also had to complete within the quarter-year a felted beret, a pair of hose with Spanish clocks and a woollen shirt. Of berets we know; we still wear them in various forms. Of hose with Spanish clocks we also know something except the reason for clocks to be so-called. Did the early decoration (used to strengthen the top point of the ankle gusset in cloth hose) look like a cluster of little bells (the origin of 'clock' being *clokke*, a

bell)? An old knitted stocking which I found in Bergen had a very bell-like ornament knitted in at that point.

Of woollen shirts we know rather little. They were probably undergarments and as such short-lived and not thought worth preserving. The oldest fragment which we have which might be a knitted sleeve or part of a knitted shirt was found recently in Copenhagen and dated to the seventeenth century. There are also a good number of silk waistcoats or shirts from the seventeenth century and some little cotton jackets. These are not traditional knitting in the sense of 'folk' knitting, but many of their features can be traced into early folk knitting and some are still used today!

From the middle of the 19th century, these Fair Isle Tammies show an unusual method of knitting from the crown out to the brim. In traditional Fair Isle colours: indigo, madder, gold and white. (From the National Museum of Antiquities of Scotland)

Knitting in Fashion

Many textile collections in Europe contain silk shirts dated usually to the seventeenth century. Some are quite plain, in one colour, with all-over patterns in purl stitch (such an elegant pale-blue shirt, in which Charles I is said to have gone to his execution, is in the Museum of London). A rather similar shirt in red is preserved in Copenhagen. Similar purl patterns were used on the very finely knitted and greatly treasured seventeenth-century vests or undershirts (cotton was a new and popular fibre). The second and more spectacular type of shirt is made up from panels of brocade knitting in several colours of silk, often with a gold thread worked in as well. The patterns are large and floral and the panels differ in the way they have been made up, some with extra flounces or later shaping or rows of buttons to adapt to changing fashions. Some contemporary capes were made of similar knitted panels sewn together and must have looked very grand.

Where were they made? The English state firmly that the brocade shirts come from Venice; the Venetians have nothing similar. The Scandinavians believe theirs were imported from England and it is said that the oldest specimens are those in southern France and Spain. All of this may be true without any contradictions; indeed, so many different styles can be identified that it is very unlikely that they were all made at one place, at one time or even by one method.

The best knitting is in the plainest shirts. That

This silk jacket is described as Elizabethan but is more likely to be 17th century, possibly altered in the 18th to give gathered sleeves and the fashionable pleated side-vents. Knitted in yellow silk and gold thread with a design (in purl) in beige and gold. The detail (overleaf) is from the side seam where two decorated selvedges are sewn together. (Photos by Burrell Collection, Glasgow)

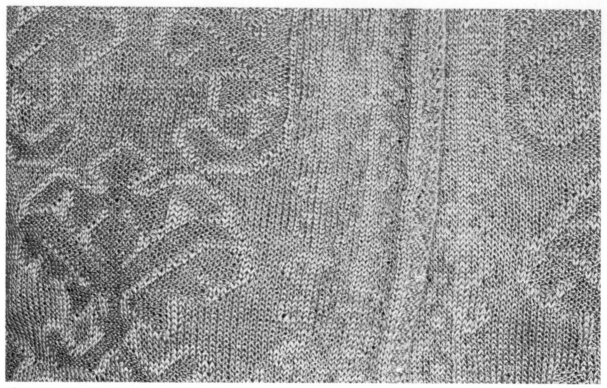

Above *Detail of jacket on page 21.*

Right *The yoke from a rare white Eriskay gansie shows patterns found in Scotland and England — like the fishermen who wore them, they worked their way around the coasts. From the armhole there is a ladder, St Andrew's Cross above a Tree of Life; zig-zags (from the paths up cliffs); and two windows, one empty and one filled. They are separated by a small version of the sand pattern. Below the nets are vertical patterns: marriage lines (or the ups and downs of married life) and crosses and diamonds separated by little ropes or cables. This extraordinary gansie weighs more than 1 kg (2½ lb). It has underarm gussets, a high ribbed neck and side openings which button forward on the left with silver buttons. Other gansie patterns include steps; print o' the hoof, a double cable; hit and miss it, moss stitch; double moss; sand and shingle, double and single moss; honeycomb; herringbone, or feather, or hen's claw; rig and fur (garter stitch ridges and furrows used on shoulder straps and shown here); waves. Scottish gansies often had simple vertical panels with columns of zig-zags, hearts, anchors, the flag or kilt, or crosses and diamonds. The Eddystone lighthouse figures on Cornish gansies.*

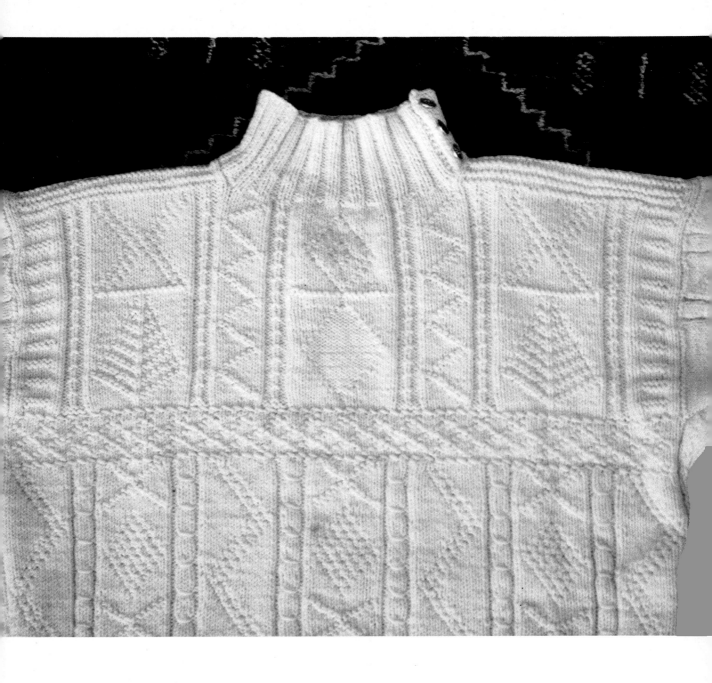

23

worn by King Charles is probably English. Some of those in Scandinavia look very different as the original pattern is completely or partly covered with later embroidery which ignores it. They often have a fleecy lining darned in as well. Under this camouflage, however, they emerge as basically plain shirts with a purl pattern.

The 'brocade' knitting by contrast is rather loose and slipshod. These jackets (or waistcoats — Pepys in 1666 was wearing a 'thin silke waistcoate') have been put together from five flat panels, each decorated along all its edges so that side seams and shoulder joins are very ornamental. They are obviously a commercial product, making up in fashionable appeal (and they *are* beautiful) what they lack in craftsmanship, and were probably the products of small commercial workshops using early hand-frames (a working prototype existed already in 1589). Italy seems as likely a source as any. In the eighteenth century Venetian frame-knitters complained about unfair competition from hand-knitters. Only by producing such expensive work could the use of the frames have been justified. We can imagine each knitter with his standard charts in front of him producing packages of panels for someone else to sew up — possibly the eventual wearer. The patterns on these silk shirts show great variations in individual style, much as one finds today in comparing cashmere sweaters from different firms. Almost all have a self-coloured lower border decorated with a diced pattern in plain and purl squares. The other selvedges in each piece have a border pattern or a series of small patterns and the space in the centre is filled in with large floral motifs. Perhaps to allow for different sizes there are odd plain sections at the tops of sleeves, with a series of patterns. As the sleeves of waistcoats showed only at the cuff in the seventeenth century,

this may have been a short-cut to save valuable gold thread.

These very glamorous silk garments link up with modern knitting in an exciting way. Quite recently as we have mentioned already, a sizeable part of a knitted sleeve was found in an excavation in Copenhagen and dated to the seventeenth century. It has an all-over pattern of diagonal lines, diamonds and eight-pointed stars. Not only is this pattern used (under all the embroidery!) for many of the silk shirts found in Scandinavia but it was knitted with very few variations for hundreds of years on the women's jackets known as *nattrøjer* (night shirts) which became an abiding part of Danish folk costume. It seems fairly certain that these jackets and their decoration go back unchanged to the

Puzzle pattern: first seen by the author in Shetland and introduced as the Sand Lodge *pattern of local invention and pre-war date, it turns up again in the commercialised Swedish knitting of around 1910 known as* Binge; *they also claim it as a local invention. However, sharp-eyed readers may have noticed a similarity between this pattern and the lower half of the Eriskay gansie in the previous illustration and indeed a vertical arrangement of zig-zags and diamonds set off by plain and purl stitches is a popular one in Scotland. Visitors to Grasmere will find a pair of gloves with a similar pattern in two colours on the back and the oldest known piece of Fair Isle knitting has a similar vertical pattern in typical Fair Isle colours. Before we claim a victory for Scotland, the Victoria and Albert Museum has a silk cap from Italy, dated to the 17th century and decorated with double vertical zig-zags separated by diamonds and vertical lines. Truly there is nothing so new as an old knitting pattern.*

seventeenth century when they were copied from imported knitted silk jackets and probably worn by both sexes. These jackets were known as night shirts because, during cold weather, they were worn by night as well as by day (in England the poorer classes also slept in their 'waistcoats' at that time). They became very short at the end of the eighteenth century, as the Empire fashion with its high waists came in, also to persist in folk costume. But they still show a split welt decorated with a diced pattern or with garter stitch, above which are one or two small patterns and then the main decoration in purl stitch. The bodice is knitted in one piece above the welt (in true craftsmanlike style) but the 'seams' at side and shoulder are often decorated so that front and back look as if they were separate knitted panels. The wool used is often indigo blue, as in the seventeenth century piece, or bright red or dark green, very finely spun and burnished in use to look almost like silk.

To digress a little, there is certainly a link here also with guernseys or gansies, the purl-patterned fishermen's 'frocks' or 'shirts' which most people now would think of as 'jerseys', not entirely correctly. In the original Guernsey style, this garment is tunic-length, with a split welt in garter stitch. We will come back to gansies later, but in knitting, as in any other technique, very little happens in isolation, and patterns seem to have moved around in the seventeenth, eighteenth and nineteenth centuries just as they do today.

Such firm links between the few valuable and fashionable knitted garments which have survived and the vast but even more transient world of folk knitting are few, simply because knitting wears out and is thrown away or, in thrifty households, recycled. But folk costumes are notoriously conservative and folk knitting patterns may preserve much older patterns once fashionable and long forgotten by the world which first invented them.

As a relatively new craft, knitting has borrowed patterns wholesale whenever decoration was wanted, either in two colours or in purl-and-plain. Embroidery of various angular types, weaving, simple carpet and lace patterns, all have been pressed into service. The modern Faeroese patterns seem to be originally ornamental darning or small damask patterns. Norwegian Selbu knitting, with its famous stars, dancing ladies, deer and other delights, is known to be copied from local traditional needlework. Estonian gloves show this very clearly as the early ones are embroidered with patterns which were later knitted in Shetland copies, while Shetland knitting of Fair Isle type has gathered patterns from every possible source and adapted them to stranded knitting with unfailing practical skill.

Knitting for a Living

Our knowledge of the traditional patterns and methods of early knitting is slight but there is no doubt that in the seventeenth and eighteenth centuries hand-knitting became a cottage industry of great economic importance in many areas of Britain and Europe. The Yorkshire Dales, Cumbria, Aberdeenshire, Shetland, the Channel Islands and elsewhere where there was a substantial rural population and, in the early days at least, suitable local wool, began to produce and export vast quantities of hand-knitted stockings, mittens, gloves, nightcaps, bonnets, waistcoats (long-sleeved and worn at night as well as by day), leggings and undergarments. Some was very coarse and 'most nastily made' as a French visitor to Aberdeenshire noted. Some, on the other hand, was knitted on needles no thicker than sewing needles with wool spun as fine as human hair and was more highly priced than silk.

But the bulk of this enormous domestic activity was aimed at the production of coarse stockings. In the early days merchants limited themselves to collecting the finished products. Soon, as demand increased and outstripped local wool supply, merchants became woollen brokers, buying in suitable raw wool and exchanging it for finished goods. In every part of the world where such a system has been set up, the same has happened - knitters knit on larger and larger needles, they use single yarn instead of double, they throw in the coarse wool with the fine, they surreptitiously stretch finished stockings a size or two larger, and put away as much of the merchant's wool as possible for private use. Eventually standards were set up: for example, wool must be 2-ply, men's hose must be at least 34 inches long and the feet fully 'Twelve Inches in Length from the Heel to the Toe and from Four and a Half to Five Inches in Breadth'. This apparently massive size is to compensate for the subsequent fulling or felting, usually combined

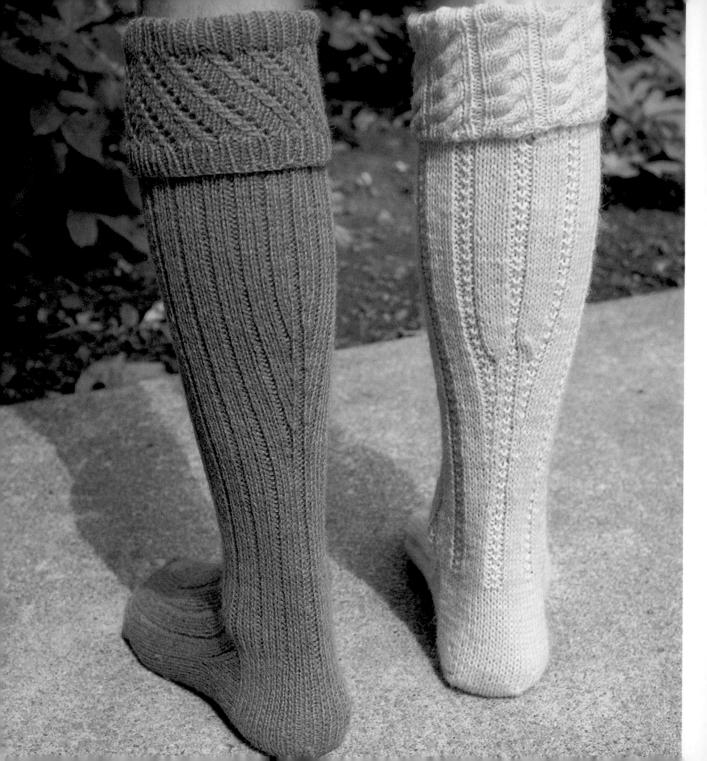

with dyeing and shaping, and in later years done by the merchant to ensure better quality control.

Whole populations — old, young, male, female, firm and infirm — took to knitting. As in Shetland still today toddlers would be given little sets of needles to learn how to hold the needles and play at knitting. By the age of four they would be knitting for practice;by the age of seven they would be spinning and knitting for sale. People knitted indoors and out, walking to market and home again, herding, sitting in sheltered corners by the sea, at social gatherings, even, it is said, at executions. They

Left *Kilt hose: a modern use for an old style; ribbed and seamed for fit, decorated tops to cover the garter, there are as many styles as there are good knitters. Here in Lovat with French heel; white with Dutch heel.*

knitted as a God-given way to make ends meet in times when the poor were the corncern of very few people. Already in 1606 the Royal Court of Jersey tried to forbid knitting of stockings during the six weeks of harvest and seaweed gathering (both essential to the survival of the island) on pain of imprisonment on bread and water. In, Yarmouth people who were found knitting on the streets were

Below *A medley of traditional Norwegian patterns. These brilliantly patterned caps, mittens and stockings are mainly from the western coast of Norway but are now known all over the world. It was only gradually that 'two-end knitting' (knitting with two strands of the same colour) to stranded knitting with colourful patterns. The object is the same: to stay twice as warm. (From the Bergen Museum)*

liable to be arrested. Gatherings of knitters in the evenings were popular not only in England and Scotland but in Norway. They may have appeared convivial and even riotous but the primary object was to save heat and light (to find a ball of wool in the dark, it was wound around a hollow rattle containing a few dried peas). Courting was a secondary object, in Shetland at least, and with the gift of country folk for making an enjoyable occasion out of a necessary chore, these knitting parties were doubtless an important part of the social life of a district. They were revived in Sweden as late as 1910 and in Finland during World War II. Non-knitters imputed great moral dereliction to those who attended knitting parties. It is, however, difficult to see how much misconduct could occur when the hands of everyone present were so fully

Above These very fine Fair Isle gloves have enough pattern for a couple of modern jerseys. The zig-zags and lines (see page 24) are out in full force on the back and the palm is even more elaborate.

Right Granny's lumber: the brightest and best for the favourite grandchild! Shetland grandmothers would be ashamed to copy a pattern. Every child is different and precious and so gets an entirely individual creation.

occupied.

Knitters often used finely carved 'knitting sticks' to hold the right-hand needle - these holders were often betrothal presents and their use left the right hand free to move the wool and knit more rapidly; it also tended to bend wire needles into a typical

shape. Needles were also held by bundles of tightly bound straw or quills or a pad of horsehair (in Shetland today).

Knitting became an important part of most families' domestic chores, especially in areas where a few sheep were kept (a more useful animal than the later household cow, in that it supplied wool as well as milk and meat). They knitted a great variety of articles for their own use, of better quality, one suspects, than those knitted for the merchant. What they knitted and what it looked like we have almost no idea beyond lists of names of garments.

In spite of the apparent difficulty of controlling an industry with so many outworkers, it was a well-organised trade and a very profitable one, with exports going from Aberdeen (one of the better documented areas) to the Netherlands for distribution on the Continent, and to Bergen and Virginia as well as to London. Throughout the 1790s the annual value of the hand-knitted stockings exported from Aberdeen was £100,000. This does not take account of those sold locally or sent to London. Local wool was no longer sufficient; by 1778 £40,000's worth of suitable wool was being bought in from London and fine fleece from Shetland also used.

When this trade declined, it did so dramatically and with finality. The reasons were several and they coincided: the loss of the American market, disruption by wars in Europe, competition from Jersey, Guernsey and Germany and, last but not least, the invention of an improved stocking-frame made economical by machine-spun yarn. Within a few years the Aberdeenshire stocking-trade had collapsed. Here and there stockings were still knitted by hand or on small machines. There was a final reverse when fashion in the early nineteenth century decreed that ladies' skirts should completely cover their ankles (to the great regret of many) and that gentlemen should henceforth wear trousers rather than the more shapely and elegant breeches and hose (also to the regret of many). When the army followed fashion, the great days of the hosiery trade were over.

It had had its moments all the same. For a long time in Shetland the annual fair was remembered with great nostalgia. All year the knitting piled up in the crofters' cottages, saved for the few weeks in the summer when the Dutch fishing-fleet arrived, to pack the Sound of Bressay with wooden boats carrying fine linen, wheaten flour, strong liquor and sometimes even sheep. A temporary camp of turf bothies grew up where Lerwick now stands and the entire annual production of knitting was bartered. Something of a carnival atmosphere developed, helped, no doubt, by the strong liquor. The first record of this early trade fair seems to be 1610 and it continued, with gaps caused by distant wars (usually about trade) until 1712 when the Salt Tax stopped the visits from foreign fishermen. Thereafter knitting was done for merchants. The Shetlanders long remembered this brave time, the year-long anticipation and the opportunities for individual profit-taking.

I have said that the great days of the hosiery trade ended when Victorian skirts reached the floor; not quite! In remote Shetland they have survived to the present day though 'hosiery' there now includes lace shawls, Fair Isle jerseys and everything else that man and woman can knit. We will come back to the Shetland hosiery trade in due course.

Knitting in the Drawing Room

Ankles retired and stockings disappeared from view, but new fashions arose to keep knitting needles busy. The poor hand-knitters, now poorer than ever, turned to coarse worsted vests (sleeved jackets or waistcoats) for seagoing men (the original jumpers) and blue woollen bonnets, commonly worn by working men and boys. In 1842 a knitter was being paid 3 pence or 4 pence for a jacket and 1 or 2 pence for a bonnet, including the wool.

Here and there some local traditions of a finer sort lingered on — the patterned gloves of Yorkshire and Dumfriesshire, the brightly striped fishermen's caps from Shetland. But it was a hard time for knitters and their craft.

Little girls today often wear white stockings with lacy patterns. It is not a coincidence that many folk costumes from one end of Europe to the other also include white stockings with lacy patterns. In Norway these are heavy, and felted, cabled rather than lacy and very warm. In Portugal they are only leggings which tie under the foot, an adaptation of a town fashion to country use. The origin of all this white knitting is the same — the white knitting of the short days of the French Empire. White wool has never been very popular in folk knitting which preferred white cotton or linen. Hand-knitters became expert lace knitters early in the nineteenth century as lace samplers from the period show. Lace knitting became a drawing-room hobby, taught to little girls at dame-schools and knitting became identified with small decorative articles, an artless way of passing the time, a suitable occupation for the aged and feeble-minded.

A genteel Edinburgh widow, Mrs Gaugain, published in mid-century three little knitting books still of great delight to those attracted by the ephemera of the craft and which show well this trivial aspect of it. Most of her patterns (many in lacework) are for small articles: a scarf, a mat, a

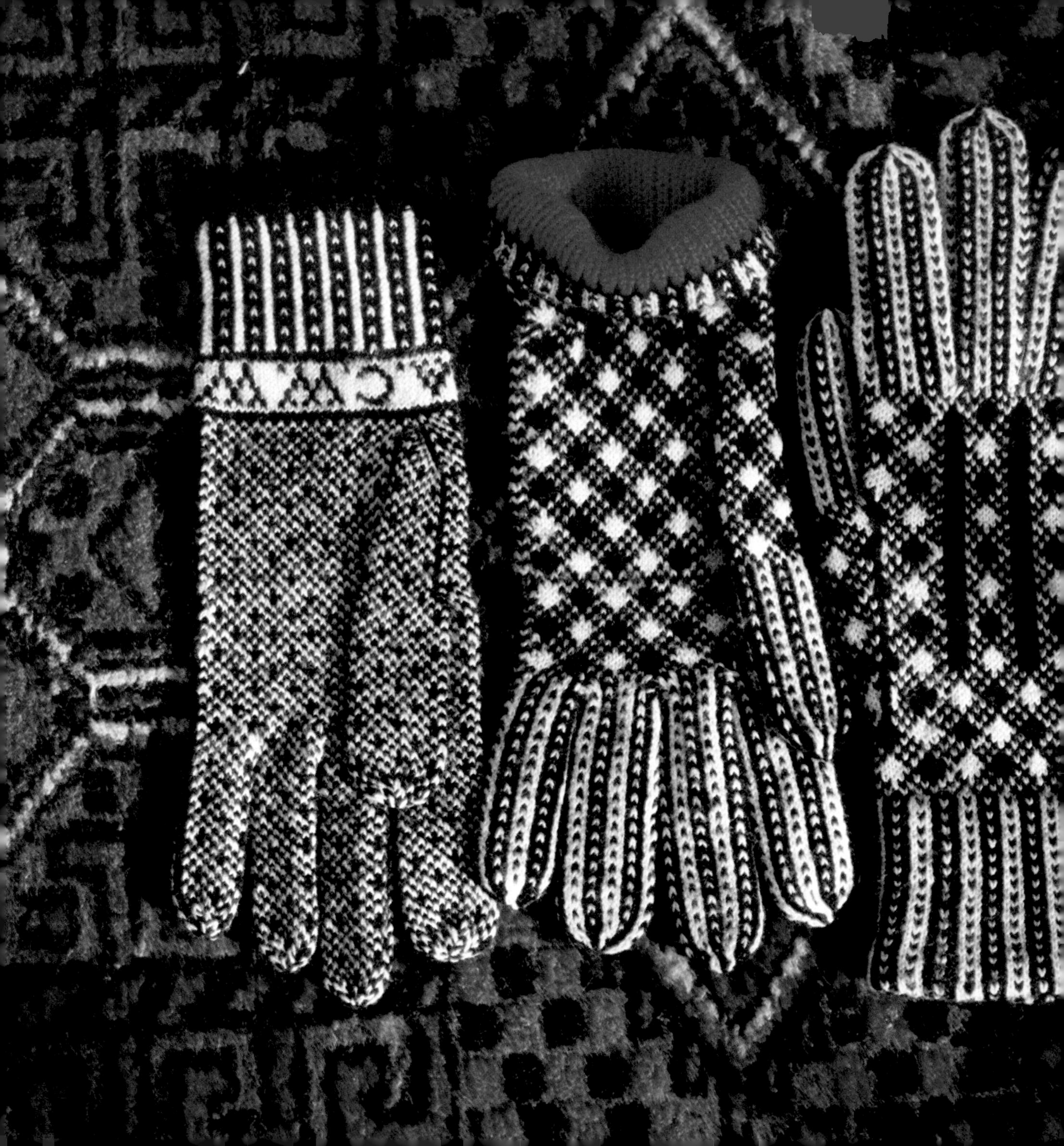

Traditional gloves: from Sanquhar, Dumfriesshire and overleaf *from the North Yorkshire Dales — a modern version knitted in Shetland. Mittens were for work; gloves for high days and holidays. Earliest patterns everywhere were in natural colours of wool — usually black and white with some russet. The Sanquhar patterns shown are: midge and fly; shepherd's plaid; duke's. Others are diamonds, small check and rose.*

35

cushion, mittens, a miniature Scotch bonnet (for holding pence), a neck band or faucett, a long purse with two rings, garters, a pincushion cover; and many copied from eighteenth century knitting. Here and there a note of realism creeps in: 'Double Knitting for Comfort', a 'Very Warm Knit Petticoat for a Lady'. A pattern is given for a child's underdress, chemise and drawers in one piece and for a child's sleeved spencer, with a discreet footnote indicating that it can easily be adapted for larger sizes.

Despite this interest in knitting, anyone who looks through Victorian photographic archives for evidence of it will be disappointed. Fishermen wear dark gansies, Scotchmen bonnets and children striped stockings; otherwise Victorian knitting was invisible and largely unrecorded.

Left *Lace sampler dated 1818.* (From the Kelvingrove Museum, Glasgow)

Above *Silk purse — Mrs Gaugain gave instructions for such a purse. The opening is in the centre and to keep your guineas safe the ring which closes off the end is first pulled up beyond the opening and then down again. Some purses had a 'gold' end for sovereigns and a 'silver' end for coins of lesser value. Floral patterns of this type are still knitted in many isolated places including Shetland, Sweden and Estonia.* (From the Kelvingrove Museum, Glasgow)

Far removed from the hard-working versions worn by farmers and fishermen, these mittens of drawing-room design show at least five different techniques: stranded knitting, intaglio, two varieties of openwork and a purl edge. The young man looks more Norwegian than English. (From the Kelvingrove Museum, Glasgow)

Knitting in the Islands

Today when people think of lace-knitting they always identify it with the incredibly fine lace shawls knitted in the nineteenth century, and since, in Shetland. That these could be passed through a wedding-ring is no myth, nor a difficult feat: a shawl measuring 2 metres square (6 feet) might weigh only 75 g (3 oz). Such fine knitting was noted much earlier in Shetland; in the eighteenth century very fine stockings were knitted and the same feat performed with them. Shetland was not the only lace-knitting centre in Europe nor the earliest — Russia and Spain were important centres and Shetland lace-knitting began around 1840. But it has an interest and a beauty entirely its own.

Simple openwork has a long history. It is one of the easiest ornamental techniques, as many young knitters discover by accident, and has been found in Burgos on gloves from 1350, and on a pair of silk stockings once worn by Queen Elizabeth of England. The old patterns, as has been mentioned, gained new emphasis when the flimsy and, to some shockingly short, muslin dresses of Empire days, allowed ladies to show more leg than ever before.

Many patterns were known: shell, lyre, leaf, honeycomb, diamond, twist, feather, round spider net, wave, wreath, van dyke. A talented lace knitter can copy almost anything.

In the early nineteenth century, every family in Shetland had been affected by the decline in demand for mass-produced hand-knitting and a variety of other handcrafts such as straw-plaiting and flax-working were introduced by philanthropic landlords who hoped thus to keep their tenants gainfully employed. The idea of knitting lace was a much more ingenious one, as it used the native wool, extraordinarily long, fine, silky and soft, a wool without peer as generations of Victorians were to find out. Several people have been credited with this brainwave, such as the Saxby family who brought lace-knitting collected in Europe up to

Unst to be copied, the start of a family industry for the Hunter family of Unst which lasted well into the twentieth century. Better documented is the story of Mr Standen who came to Lerwick on holiday in 1839 and saw some rather primitive lace-knitting. It had been copied from a christening cap sent to Lerwick as a present in 1833 and said to have been the first piece of lace-knitting seen there. Mr Standen went home to Oxford and did two vital things — he sent smooth metal 'wires' north and he introduced Shetland knitting to the London market. It was a sensational success and apparently within the year a flourishing trade had grown up. This got further impetus from the Parcel Post, introduced in 1840 — a service now taken for granted but a breakthrough which meant that after more than a century Shetland knitters could again deal directly with customers.

A beautiful example of a 'wedding-ring' shawl of Shetland design. Shawls like this were knitted in the 19th century from the finest yarn hand-spun from the neck fleece of the small native sheep. They have never been surpassed for beauty of design or craftsmanship. Such a shawl might weigh only 75 g (3 oz). (From the Kelvingrove Museum, Glasgow)

The early pieces were fairly crude, rudely executed on wooden pins. The finest shawls are today collectors' items and almost as precious as the silk shirts; fragile and feather-light, they were never everyday items and many have been safely kept. They were, however, only one very specialised product. Once the delight of Shetland wool, as soft and warm as silk, had been appreciated by southern customers, they could not get enough of it,

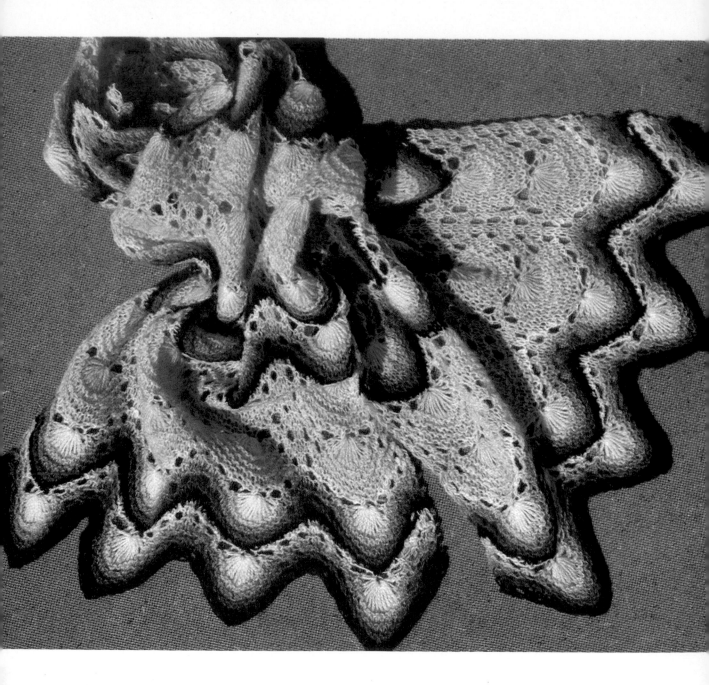

Above *Hand-spinning in Shetland: a rare photograph of a once-universal sight, a crofter spinning her own wool beside a peat fire with the traditional backstone to reflect the heat. Her wheel is the Shetland type, first used for flax but equally suitable for wool.* (Photo by J. Lamotte)

Left *Modern Shetland scarf in a traditional pattern and traditional colours.*

especially for underwear. Everyday openwork shawls known as 'haps' were knitted for local use and for sale, usually in the darker colours of the family sheep: greys, fawns, 'Shetland black' and moorit (a rich brown-red, a glorious colour and much prized).

Lace-knitting was the mainstay of the Shetland knitting industry throughout the second half of the nineteenth century. It had its drawbacks for knitters. Spinning had still to be done by hand to produce the fine single-ply yarn and this, and the knitting, made very fine hands essential. For this reason the finest work was generally done by the more delicate women who were in any case less able for the normal heavy work of the croft. The sedentary nature of their occupation often made their health worse, as improving tracts of the time suggest, without, however, giving any reasonable alternative ways of earning a living. Handicapped or invalid men also knitted, as in other places and at other times. They are said not to have been so good at it nor so neat but happy enough if they could make enough to barter for tobacco (this is from Norway, not from Shetland, but knitters are knitters the world over).

This system of barter or 'truck' rather than selling

Dressing hosiery in Shetland: two jerseys and an openwork scarf stretched to proper shape and left to dry in the fresh air. Natural wool will always benefit from being firmly stretched over a frame when washed. Frames were made for gloves, jerseys, shawls, the various sizes of stockings and even for long johns. (Photo by J. Lamotte)

for cash was a source of much misery in Shetland and led eventually to the passing of the Truck Acts in the 1880s, an unanticipated legacy of which has been to delay payment by cheque in this country, for, as any personnel manager will tell you, the Truck Acts can still be invoked by any employee who wishes to be paid in cash. The drawback in Victorian times came from the fact that in most country parishes there was only one shop or booth, where knitting was bought and knitting-wool and

groceries sold. Unscrupulous merchants were not slow to use their monopoly to their advantage. To those without family responsibilities, however, it seems to have mattered little. Country girls cheerfully bartered everything they knitted for incongruous imported finery which they wore to church on Sunday, this being the only social occasion where such garments could be displayed to advantage.

Knitting for home consumption was more for comfort and less for style. The wool was plucked, not sheared, once a year when the natural growth of the new wool loosened the old. Plucking is recorded from many other countries in Europe and the Middle East. The wool thus gathered has no short, sharp pieces and no cut ends and is wonderfully kind to the skin. The fleece was carefully sorted, as each animal produced wool of different qualities. The best wool was always laid aside for the jupies (jumpers) worn by the seagoing men of the family under their oilskins. The coarsest was used for bed-rugs and rough stockings, often felted. Grey wool was preferred for men's stockings and moorit wool for women's. I was once shown with great pride an old scarf laid away carefully in a croft in Fladdabister. It was generously deep, finished off with long fringes and knitted in soft moorit wool. The wool had come from the distant forefathers of the sheep who still grazed outside, though today few of them are brown and all are clipped.

To us now it seems curious that for a long time knitting was deliberately felted. Today all our endeavours are to avoid that unhappy process. When all the processes were done by hand, however, it was desirable to have an end-product which lasted as long as possible, besides being weather-proof and warm, and felting achieved all these desirable things. Felting was applied to caps in Tudor times and to caps such as the beret today. It was applied to jackets which could then be tailored and trimmed. The navy jackets worn by Faeroese men are knitted, though it is not easy to see this. Most of the stockings ever made have been felted, dyed and shaped in one operation.

Merchant's booth: the modern Shetland equivalent of the old merchant's trading booth; a combined wool shop and retail outlet for hand-knitting. (Photo by J. Lamotte)

Fair Isle Knitting

In 1890 there was a herring boom in Shetland and, as in boom times since, knitting suddenly became old-fashioned, a by-gone industry to list with straw-plaiting, kelp-burning and flax-working. The great days of the herring trade seem to have made little impact on Fair Isle, an outlying island to the south, where people had been knitting strange, wonderful, brilliant patterns for as long as the Lerwick ladies had been engrossed in lace. To the Victorians this early Fair Isle must have seemed literally wild and wonderful; I wonder if these early pieces were ever worn. Even today the colours dazzle.

There seems to be no truth whatsoever in a Spanish or, even less plausible, a Viking origin to Fair Isle knitting. The Spanish story dates back to a Victorian flight of fancy in 1856; the Viking idea is an even more absurd modern myth. The first Fair Isle knitting was seen in 1851 and probably owes its existence to a similar benevolent influence from outside as we have seen in the lace-knitting story.

The Fair Isle memory, and I would rely a lot on a Fair Isle memory, is that a sailor returning home from foreign parts brought back a shawl, a fashionable present in 1840 or so, and the women of Fair Isle tried, with some success, to copy it in knitting.

This jersey was probably knitted in Fair Isle around 1900. The great variety of patterns, collected from old Fair Isle patterns, Scottish Fleet patterns and apparently from Faeroe or Norway, are unified by the unvarying Fair Isle colour scheme: bands of madder red with natural white and alternating indigo blue or natural brown with vegetable-dyed gold using one of the local plants. Indigo-dyed wool was always at a premium; thrifty housewives eked it out by carefully substituting the naturally coloured wool of the 'black' sheep (in fact dark brown). (Photo by the National Museum of Antiquities of Scotland, Edinburgh)

An early Shetland copy of a Fair Isle scarf with typical large Fair Isle lozenge-and-cross patterns alternating with smaller border patterns — these small patterns are very old. Natural brown and shop-bought blue wool have been used. (From the Shetland Museum)

There must be more to it, however. Fair Isle then was a miserably poor and deprived island, unbelievably crowded (350 souls on 1½ square miles) and with few resources other than the seas around it. Fair Isle patterns have always used imported indigo, madder and possibly cochineal, not the older native vegetable dyes. These imported dyes have been known in parts of mainland Scotland for hundreds of years but apparently did not reach Mainland Shetland until around 1820. Fair Isle was relatively less isolated in those days than it is today but had few visitors and no regular ferry service. Maybe they traded for indigo with passing ships; maybe some benevolent visitor arranged for a regular supply. Some degree of organisation has been necessary to get Fair Isle knitting going in its place of origin; more than that we cannot say.

Nor, despite years of searching, can I say that I know where the shawl came from. I think I know what it may have looked like but I have learned to have considerable reservations about my knowledge of early Fair Isle. I can only say that woven patterns with about the right style and degree of complexity can be found in Estonia in the nineteenth century, that Estonians were knitting colourful and complex stranded patterns quite early in that century and that at the same time there was considerable trade between Shetland and the Baltic, particularly for timber. Moreover, exported pieces of Estonian knitting turn up here and there — a cap in the Shetland Museum, a pair of gloves in Copenhagen, Estonian patterns in Denmark and in Aran. The oldest pieces of knitting (a matching cap and purse in the National Museum of Antiquities of Scotland) which show typical Fair Isle patterns are in silk, not the bright, home-spun wool of Fair Isle. The cap at any rate is similar to knitted caps worn by Estonian women in the nineteenth century. Is this our imported 'shawl', or were several different types of pattern copied at once? The origin of the Fair Isle patterns is still a mystery.

As in any study all we can safely rely on are what we can see and what we can read (with reservations for the latter) and what we see of Fair Isle knitting is remarkable enough. That this isolated hilly island, battered by some of the wildest and foggiest seas in creation, could produce knitting with such a wealth of pattern and colour that the world is still learning from it, is surely one of the most amazing stories in any craft.

Shetland Trader jersey: a designer-inspired style which uses all the old patterns in subtle combinations of naturally coloured wool. Outworkers who knitted such jerseys for the Shetland Trader *in the 1970s soon began to copy them for their private customers and so another new trend in traditional knitting took root.*

Gansie Knitting

Gansies are as old a tradition as we find in European knitting. Similar dark-dyed, patterned, closely knit jackets, sometimes felted, often not, seem to have been worn around the coasts of the North Sea since the seventeenth century at least. Ladies from the Dutch-Danish districts of Amager in Denmark wore similar sleeves sewn on to cloth bodices. Their patterns are different, though still knitted in purl, but as knitting was considered too menial a task for such wealthy farm-wives, it was done for them by Swedish maids who came over as farm-servants. Did they bring patterns with them from further east? Or did they take Dutch patterns back with them? The second seems more likely as similar styles are found in parts of the Netherlands, and Dutch folk costume is in general most resistant to change.

Gladys Thomson and others have done knitting great service by recording the old patterns and local traditions while these were still alive. While plain gansies were always popular, there is a sound practical reason behind the patterns: the various purl-and-plain varieties, cables and ribs all had one purpose which was to make the fabric firmer, thicker and warmer. In Scotland cables were less popular as they were thought to weaken the softer wool used there and to shorten its life.

Regional variations certainly existed although most patterns were as widely spread as the fishermen themselves. But very often in one village there would be one or two ladies who earned a modest living by knitting gansies for other families. Their style, like that of the Betty Martin whose stitch is still used in the north-east, would be easily identifiable and could be regarded as traditional for that village. More significance than that has to be regarded as another modern myth. A practical application was unfortunately not a modern invention. In areas where inshore rather than deep-sea fishing was carried on, local patterns made it easier to identify the bodies of those who were

inevitably lost at sea. A man could no more wear the gansie of the next village than he could change his name; he might then suffer the ultimate fate of being buried among strangers.

Knitting for merchants was also done, with the entire female side of the family involved. The merchants provided the yarn, the youngest girls did the rib, the older girls worked the plain part up to the armholes and mother did the patterns and finished off the shoulders. The yarn, needless to say, was made to go as far as possible so that a little might be left over for the family's private use. Finished gansies might be judiciously stretched by being put damp under a cushion or through the mangle, all time-worn ploys. Suspicious merchants sometimes weighed the returned goods. Meanwhile the younger boys in the family wore variegated gansies in every shade of blue.

The living tradition of Aran patterns — chunky, white, each one different from every other, covered with cables, twists, travelling stitches, ribs, honeycombs and bobbles, they probably date back only to the early years of the 20th century. Many patterns are the same as other coastal 'gansies', others are also found in Norway and Austria, perhaps independent discoveries, perhaps not. White wool was seldom used in folk knitting, it being considered poor and shameful, except where it did not show. Regarding the ancient origin of the Aran pattern as supposedly demonstrated in the Book of Kells, I cannot do better than add the comment of one reviewer who pointed out that even the sheep seem to be wearing knitted body-stockings.

Popular Knitting

Textile historians from future ages will look back on the twentieth century as the time when knitting finally came of age. Nothing in common wear today is taken so much for granted and is yet as surprising as the jersey. Its forerunner was worn only by fishermen and peasants; as a long-sleeved undergarment it was so unfashionable that it went by dozens of aliases: vest, undervest, waistcoat, underwaistcoat, spencer, semmit, sark, wylie-coat, undershirt, jupie, jumper, petticoat — to unravel these names is to unravel most of the history of dress over five hundred years. Now the entire population wears woollies for all but the most solemn occasions and is year by year encroaching there as well.

This popularity has had drawbacks, however. World War I gave renewed importance to hand-knitting, as wars have often done in the past, but the old skills had been neglected. As quantity was seen to be more important than quality, the most dreadful printed patterns appeared in large numbers. World War II produced even more and worse knitting instructions. Far from increasing production they must have slowed it down for, forgetting that knitting is a circular technique, everything, even fingers of gloves, had to be knitted in small rectangles and then sewn up. Knitting still suffers from this basic lack of understanding, more on the part of knitting designers than on the part of good knitters. Shetland knitters will smile and shake their heads in sympathy if a visitor complains that

Scandinavian sweater in natural white and russet (perhaps madder or a lichen dye). This marvellous piece of entirely seamless knitting is possibly Faeroese, though if anyone has better information I would be delighted to have it. The raglan-look sleeves are in fact a continuous yoke. (From the Scottish Women's Rural Institutes, Edinburgh)

Such mittens are traditional all over Scandinavia
(right to left), *from Iceland, Norway and Finland.*

Fair Isle patterns are difficult to knit — 'not', they say, 'if you keep the right side facing you'. Until knitters (and designers) forget to knit in flat pieces and begin to think of knitting as a circular craft again, its potential will remain largely unrealised.

Traditional knitting has given today's knitters a great deal. Almost every pattern printed, whether the designers realise it or not, derives from an older traditional idea — diagonally quilted textures, cables and ribs, Aran braids and honeycombs, circular yokes, polonecks, innumerable Fair Isle and lace and other fancy stitches. Ski caps, knickerbocker stockings, scarves and mittens have all come into use straight from folk knitting, but the development of the jersey is a more remarkable story.

About the middle of the nineteenth century jerseys seem to have developed spontaneously in certain isolated places: Estonia had multi-coloured

Above *A new style in 1860, this Norwegian coastal jersey was worn with high-waisted trousers, an early form of dungaree, and the lower part, which was unseen, could be knitted in plain white. This saved precious dyed wool and the knitter's reputation. Setesdal jerseys also have a white welt and fishermen's caps as far apart as Sweden and Fair Isle use white for linings and inside the double-folded brim.* (From the Bergen Museum)

Right *Leg-warmers. Traditional Finnish socks are long, colourful and decorated with a whole succession of cheerful patterns added on as the knitter thought of them. Some have patterns only at the top, where they would show above boots, with a row of little hearts as the last pattern, half-hidden. Footless leggings were popular in the Baltic, usually worn with short plain socks. This is a modern use for an old idea.*

felted jackets, Faeroe plain navy ones. Delsbo and Halland in Sweden, Setesdal and Fana in Norway, Korsna in Finland all began to knit very differently patterned jerseys. The Norwegian ones were black and white, the others brightly coloured and sometimes crocheted as well as knitted. The ideas do not come from local knitting; they seem to have been invented out of thin air. Iceland at that time produced very loosely knitted jerseys using the coarse hairy part of the wool of the local sheep. With 4½ stitches to the inch they look quite casual and modern. The jerseys of Fair Isle are a rather late development (around 1900) but second to none of the others in brilliance of design and colour. The main reason for their late development was probably the shortage till then of adequate supplies of suitable wool. Aran jerseys cannot be traced much before 1906 (when the islanders wore 'ordinary' navy gansies). Their development, together with all the varieties of yoked jerseys — Fair Isle, Icelandic, Norwegian — and many others, has been in this century. Are these ideas traditional? Perhaps not yet, but they are certainly folk knitting on a large scale and ideas are continually being adapted from one sphere of knitting and design to another. It is a most exciting time to be a knitting enthusiast. It is also a very profitable time to look closely at our traditional resources; they have not survived over the centuries without good practical reasons and whether we look at Shetland, Scandinavia or further afield, we will find endless ideas from the past which can be used today.

I make no apology for continually referring to Shetland — in Shetland today we get as close as we can to the heart of traditional knitting, its craftsmanship, inventiveness, vitality and sound commercial common-sense. It is worth remembering that the best Shetland knitting never leaves the islands (except on the backs of its fishermen and students) and the second-best is never seen in shops. Good knitters today are busy all year round, just as they were in the seventeenth century when the Dutch fishing fleet crowded into Lerwick Harbour.

In conclusion, knitting is in many ways an ideal craft for today. It is no longer true that it has to be economically worthwhile; it is sufficient in itself. The varying levels of skill can be explored (if knitters would only lift their eyes from their paper patterns and read a little about the basics). Not the least thing, the end result is useful as well as beautiful and, we would hope, unique.

Yoked jerseys are neat, easy to design oneself and easy to knit up. This one uses traditional Norwegian patterns and a collar in corrugated rib.

Wheel pattern tammies are perennial favourites and are easier to knit than to describe. A lot of their shape, in fact, often comes from being stretched over a plate. The fancy crowns are worked with regular double reductions (slip 2, knit 1, pass the slipped stitches over) always using two colours, and every one comes out different.

Index